Palms

Written and Illustrated by Tyler Smith

CFI • An imprint of Cedar Fort, Inc. • Springville, Utah

ISBN 13: 978-1-4621-4794-6
ebook ISBN 13: 978-1-4621-4795-3
Published by CFI, an imprint of Cedar Fort, Inc.
2373 W. 700 S., Suite 100, Springville, UT 84663
Distributed by Cedar Fort, Inc., www.cedarfort.com

Library of Congress Control Number: 2024952147

Cover design and interior layout and design by Shawnda T. Craig
Cover design © 2025 Cedar Fort, Inc.

Printed in China

10 9 8 7 6 5 4 3 2 1

Printed on acid-free paper

To Mom

for helping to plant my seed of faith.

Palm Sunday

On that first Palm Sunday, all the streets
were filled with cheers.
"Hosanna! The Lord is King! No more
sorrow! No more fears!"

Triumphantly, the Savior rode all
through the city streets.
The crowd threw clothes and
Palm leaves beneath His feet.

The children threw their hands up,
their *palms* stretched in the air—
"Hosanna to the Son of David!"
All could hear their prayer.

Then Jesus, riding by the children,
met them with his gaze,
saying, "From the mouth of babes,
the Lord perfected, praise."

He turned His face to cleanse the temple,
casting out each thief,
Then He spent His time teaching,
healing those with grief.

With His *palms*, He broke the bread;
He passed the cup of wine.
"Remember me," He gently said.
"Partake of this as a sign."

With His *palms*, He washed the feet
of every loyal friend.
Then all alone he sat and felt what
none could comprehend.

With Their Palms

Yet, with the palms of their hands,
by the ending of that week,
Soldiers bound him as a lamb
and struck Him on the cheek.

With their *palms* pointed down,
one finger extended,
They accused and condemned Him.
Every man was offended.

With their *palms*, they placed a crown
of thorns upon His head.
With their *palms*, they beat and bruised
Him; His precious blood shed.

Disciples watched their King of
Kings walk toward Calvary.
He carried His cross and as
a lamb went willingly.

With their *palms*, they grabbed the nails,
the hammer, and the spear.
And as His *palms* were stretched out wide,
He knew the end was near.

With His Palms

Then with His 𝒫𝒶𝓁𝓂𝓈 still stretched out
wide, they nailed His hands and feet.
And with His 𝒫𝒶𝓁𝓂𝓈 still stretched out wide,
He said, "It is complete."

With His *palms* he healed the blind,
the deaf, the sick, the weak.
And with His *palms* upon their heads,
He caused the mute to speak.

With His *palms*, He calmed the storms
while on the raging sea.
With His *palms*, He beckoned all,
and said, "Come follow me."

With His *palms* stretched wide,
He said, "Forgive for what they've done."
With His *palms* stretched wide,
He said, "Behold, God's only Son."

Our Savior and Redeemer knows
what no one understands.
He tells us, "I have graven thee
upon the *palms* of my hands."

With My Palms

I look to Him, with palms outstretched, with healing in His wings.
With songs of His redeeming love—He overcomes death's sting.

I bring my palms together and I kneel on bended knee.
I thank Him for the sacrifice He gave for you and me.

As I bring my palms together, pleading for my Savior's love,
I thank Him for the blessings that He sends me from above.

I promise Him my willing heart, my feet, my words, my hands.
I promise I will do my part; I'll stand where He would stand.

I ponder on the joy and peace that He has brought me.
I hope one day that I can be who He wants me to be.

So with my *palms*, I worship Him in all I say and do.
I lift and serve and bless, proclaiming what I know is true.

And with my *palms*, I point to Him and shout eternal praise.
And with my *palms* outstretched, I try to serve Him all my days.

So one day, when I see Him with His *palms* still stretched out wide,
He will say, "Well done, my child, with me, you can reside."

Then I will feel His warm embrace, his *palms* will pull me in.
I'll feel His love, His mercy, His grace when I'm freed from sin.

With His *palms*—I am delivered.
With His *palms*—I am saved.
With my *palms*—I will serve Him.
On His *palms*—I am engraved.

Author's Note

This book was inspired by several verses from the King James Version of the Bible and a few quotes from leaders of the Church of Jesus Christ of Latter-day Saints. I have included those verses and quotes below.

Isaiah 49:16
Behold, I have graven thee upon the palms of my hands; thy walls are continually before me.

Matthew 21:15–16
And when the chief priests and scribes sar the wonderful things that he did, and the children crying in the temple, and saying Hosanna to the Son of David; they were sore displeased, And said unto him, Hearest thou what these say? And Jesus saith unto them, Yea; have ye never read, Out of the mouth of babes and sucklings thou has perfected praise?

John 18:22
And when he had thus spoken, one of the officers which stood by struck Jesus with the palm of his hand, saying, Answerest thou the high priest so?

Matthew 26:67–68
Then did they spit in his face, and buffeted him; and others smote him with the palms of their hands, Saying Prophesy unto us, thou Christ, Who is he that smote thee?

President Russell M. Nelson, "The Peace and Hope of Easter" (video), April 2021.
"Make Palm Sunday truly holy by remembering, not just the palms that were waved to honor the entrance of Jesus into Jerusalem, but by remembering the palms of His hands."

Elder Ronald A. Raspband, "Hosana to the Most High God" April 2023.
"The multitude who paid tribute with palms hailed Him as the Messiah. That was exactly who He was. They were drawn to Him, His miracles, and His teachings. But the adulation for many did not last. Some who earlier had shouted, "Hosanna," soon turned and cried, "Crucify him."